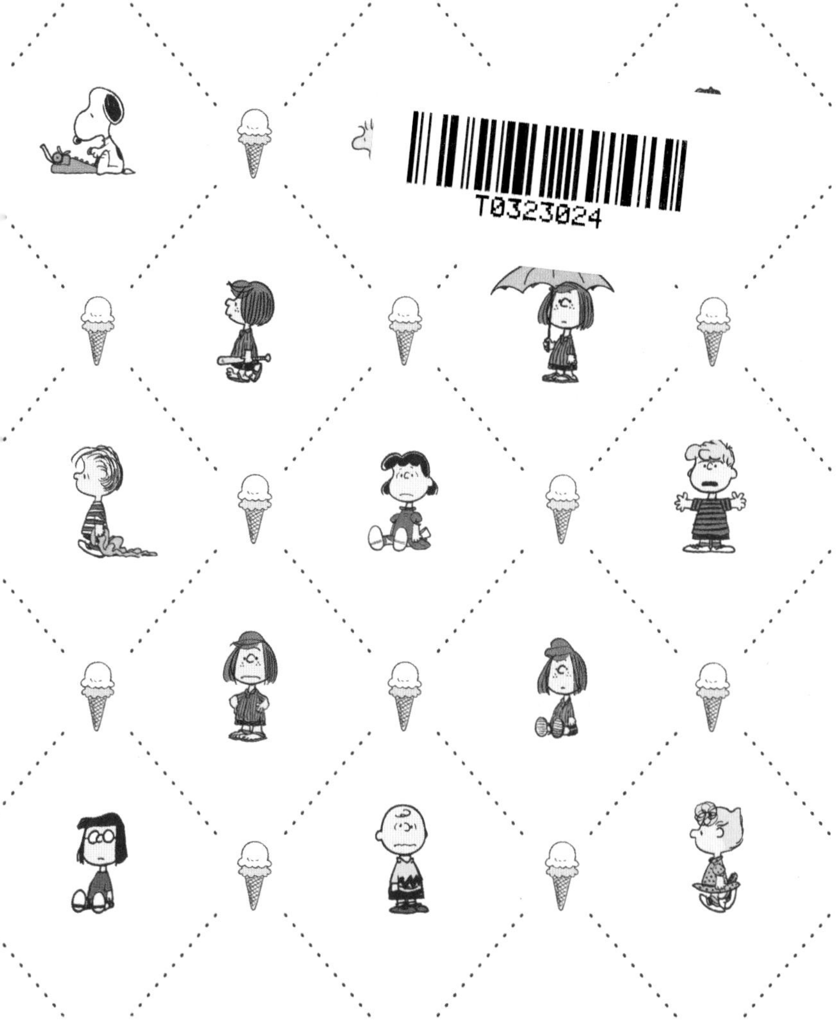

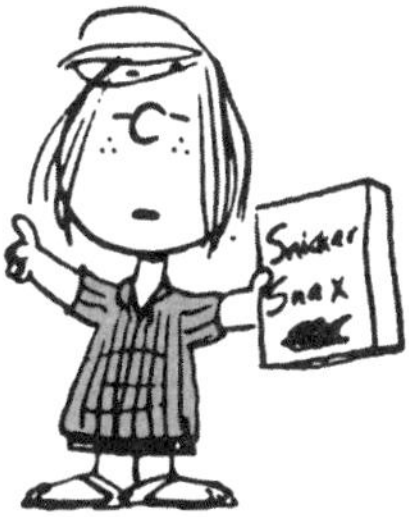
Snicker Snax

Published in Great Britain in 2016 by Canongate Books Ltd,
14 High Street, Edinburgh EH1 1TE

canongate.co.uk

2

Copyright © 2016 by Peanuts Worldwide LLC

The moral right of the author has been asserted

British Library Cataloguing-in-Publication Data
A catalogue record for this book is available on
request from the British Library

ISBN 978 1 78211 362 1

PEANUTS written and drawn by Charles M. Schulz
Edited by Jenny Lord and Andy Miller
Design: Rafaela Romaya
Layout: Stuart Polson

Printed in Italy by L.E.G.O. S.p.A.

CHARLES M. SCHULZ

THE PREDICAMENTS OF
PEPPERMINT PATTY

CANONGATE

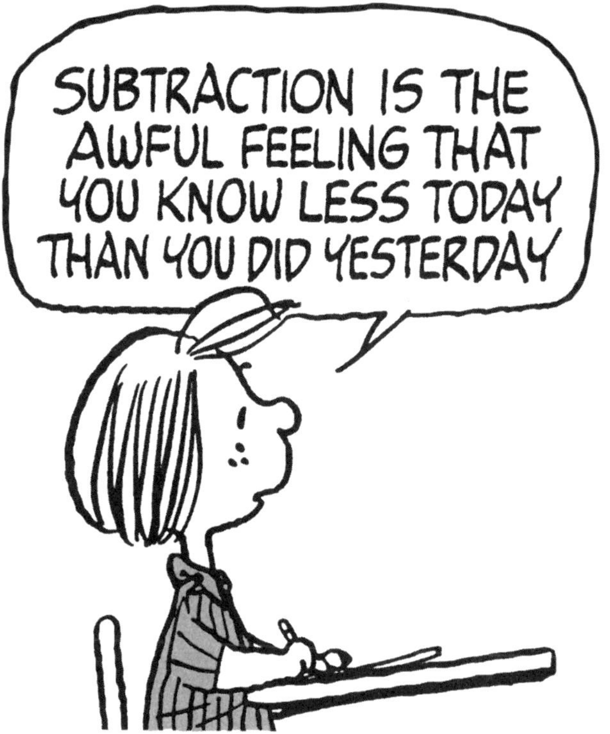
SUBTRACTION IS THE AWFUL FEELING THAT YOU KNOW LESS TODAY THAN YOU DID YESTERDAY

FOUR TIMES FOUR?
FOUR TIMES FOUR IS FORTY-FOUR!

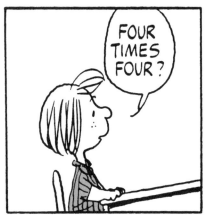

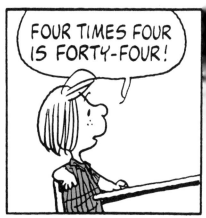

FORTY-FOUR TIMES FORTY-FOUR IS FOUR-FORTY FORTY-FOUR!
IT ISN'T? WELL, IT WAS FUN TO SAY!

GOLLY, SIR, IT'S GREAT TO SEE YOU AT CAMP AGAIN THIS YEAR
STOP CALLING ME "SIR"!
DO YOU REMEMBER ME? MY NAME IS MARCIE.. WE WERE IN THE SAME TENT LAST YEAR
OF COURSE, I REMEMBER YOU...

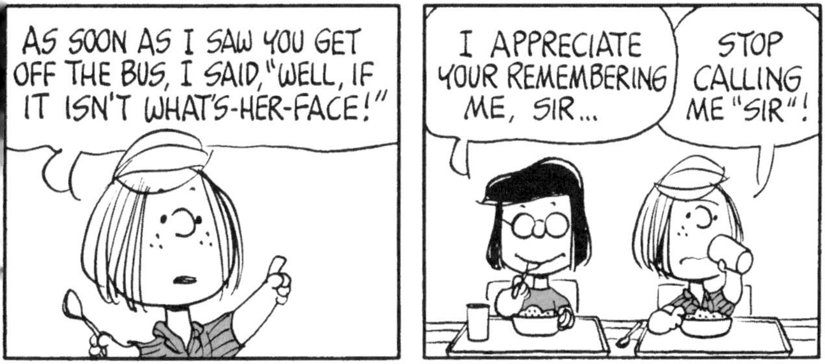
AS SOON AS I SAW YOU GET OFF THE BUS, I SAID, "WELL, IF IT ISN'T WHAT'S-HER-FACE!"
I APPRECIATE YOUR REMEMBERING ME, SIR...
STOP CALLING ME "SIR"!

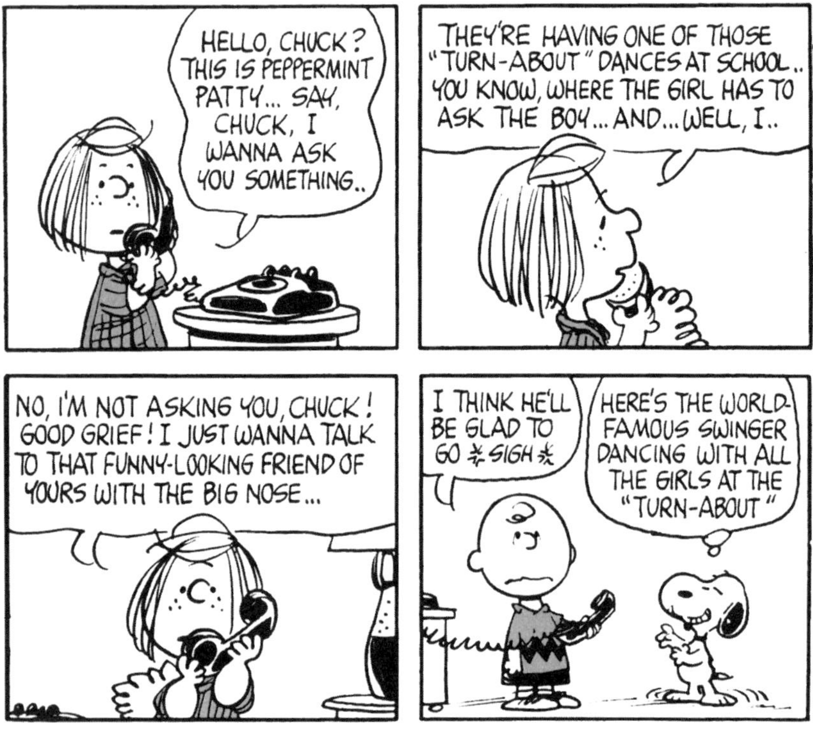
HELLO, CHUCK? THIS IS PEPPERMINT PATTY... SAY, CHUCK, I WANNA ASK YOU SOMETHING..
THEY'RE HAVING ONE OF THOSE "TURN-ABOUT" DANCES AT SCHOOL.. YOU KNOW, WHERE THE GIRL HAS TO ASK THE BOY... AND... WELL, I..
NO, I'M NOT ASKING YOU, CHUCK! GOOD GRIEF! I JUST WANNA TALK TO THAT FUNNY-LOOKING FRIEND OF YOURS WITH THE BIG NOSE...
I THINK HE'LL BE GLAD TO GO *SIGH*
HERE'S THE WORLD-FAMOUS SWINGER DANCING WITH ALL THE GIRLS AT THE "TURN-ABOUT"

BOY, SNOOPY, YOU'RE A GREAT DANCER..HOW ABOUT STOPPING FOR A LITTLE REST AND SOME COLD PUNCH?
I'M SURE GLAD YOU CAME WITH ME... I'VE NEVER HAD SO MUCH FUN IN ALL MY LIFE...I DON'T THINK ANYTHING COULD SPOIL THIS EVENING FOR ME...
PSST! HEY, KID, WHERE'D Y'GET THE WEIRD-LOOKIN' BOY FRIEND?
POW!!

HANDING IN AN ESSAY TEST WHEN YOU KNOW YOU DID TERRIBLE IS AN AWFUL FEELING..
YOU WALK BACK TO YOUR DESK, AND YOU WANT TO DIE!

EXCEPT YOU DON'T DIE.. AND IT'S ONLY OCTOBER, AND SCHOOL LASTS UNTIL JUNE, AND THERE'LL BE MORE ESSAY TESTS AND MORE AGONY, AND...
MAYBE I SHOULD TRY STUDYING...

I'M SCARED, CHUCK... WHAT IF I GROW UP, AND NO ONE EVER LOVES ME? WE PEOPLE WITH BIG NOSES ARE VERY INSECURE...
DO YOU THINK I HAVE A BIG NOSE, CHUCK? DO YOU THINK SOMEONE WILL LOVE ME SOMEDAY?
SURE
SURE?! "SURE," WHAT? "SURE" I HAVE A BIG NOSE, OR "SURE" SOMEONE WILL LOVE ME SOMEDAY?
MAYBE SOMEDAY THE REST OF YOUR FACE WILL CATCH UP WITH YOUR NOSE, AND THEN SOMEONE WILL LOVE YOU

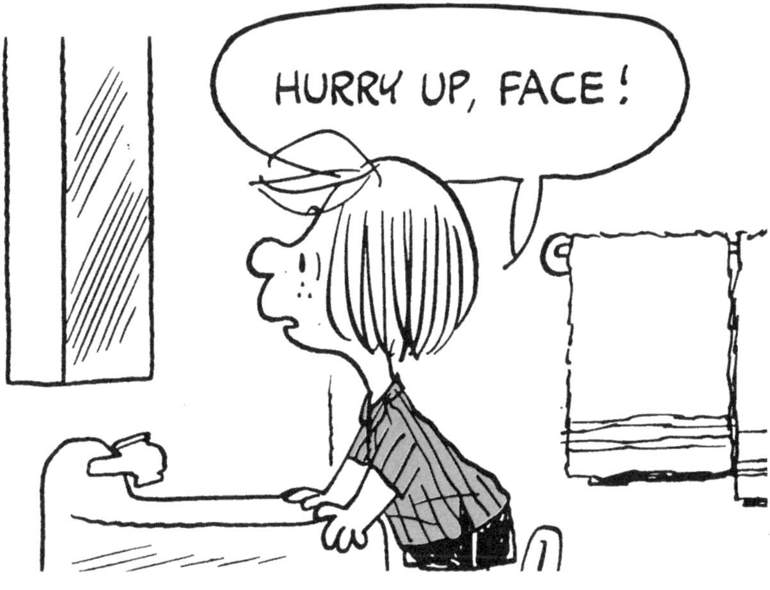
HURRY UP, FACE!

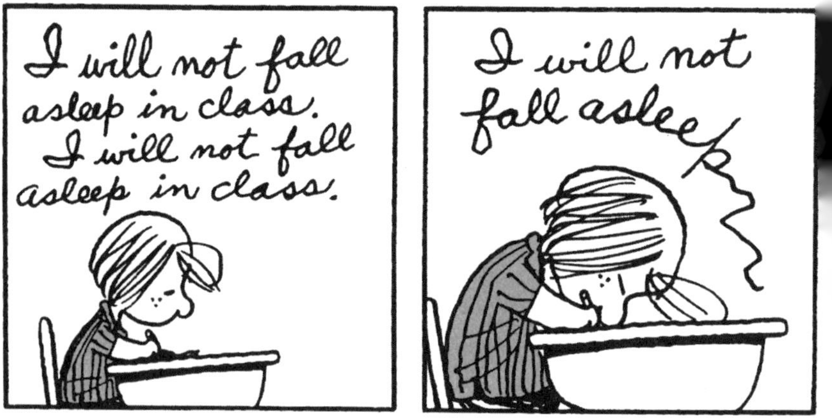
I will not fall asleep in class. I will not fall asleep in class.
I will not fall asleep

in class.

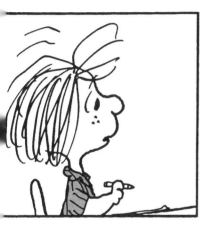

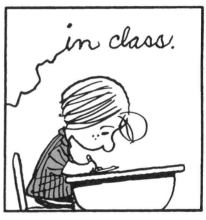

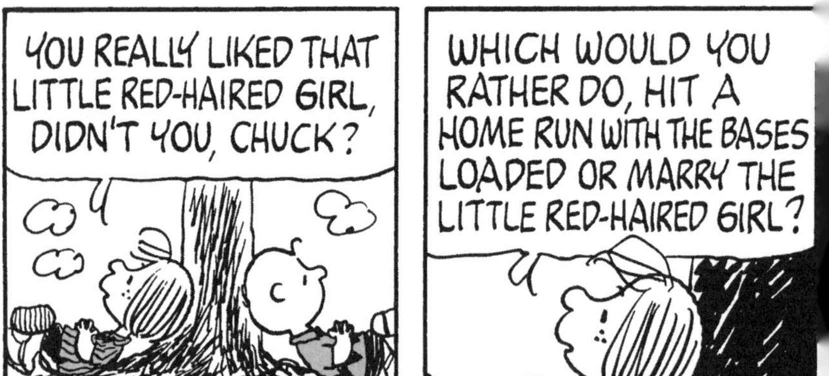
YOU REALLY LIKED THAT LITTLE RED-HAIRED GIRL, DIDN'T YOU, CHUCK?
WHICH WOULD YOU RATHER DO, HIT A HOME RUN WITH THE BASES LOADED OR MARRY THE LITTLE RED-HAIRED GIRL?

WHY COULDN'T I DO BOTH?
WE LIVE IN A REAL WORLD, CHUCK!

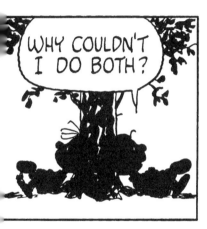

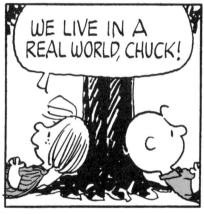

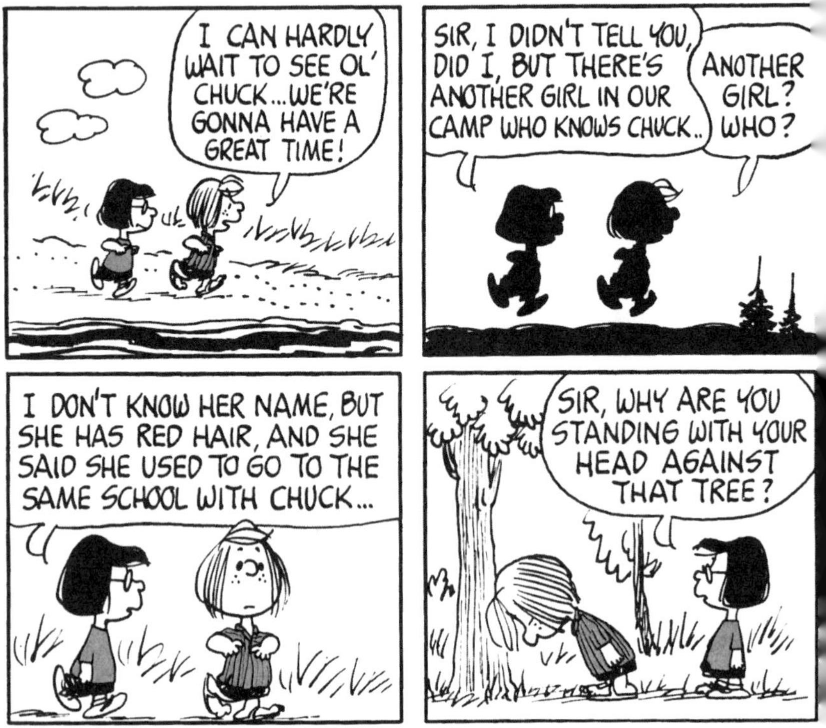
I CAN HARDLY WAIT TO SEE OL' CHUCK...WE'RE GONNA HAVE A GREAT TIME!
SIR, I DIDN'T TELL YOU, DID I, BUT THERE'S ANOTHER GIRL IN OUR CAMP WHO KNOWS CHUCK..
ANOTHER GIRL? WHO?
I DON'T KNOW HER NAME, BUT SHE HAS RED HAIR, AND SHE SAID SHE USED TO GO TO THE SAME SCHOOL WITH CHUCK...
SIR, WHY ARE YOU STANDING WITH YOUR HEAD AGAINST THAT TREE?

WHAT HAPPENED AT THE GIRLS' CAMP, PATTY?
I SAW THE LITTLE RED-HAIRED GIRL, LINUS...
I HEARD THAT SOMEONE GOT QUITE UPSET... WHAT HAPPENED?
I ACTUALLY SAW HER, LINUS...
I STOOD RIGHT IN FRONT OF HER...I FINALLY SAW THE LITTLE RED-HAIRED GIRL THAT CHUCK IS ALWAYS TALKING ABOUT.. AND YOU KNOW WHAT I DID?
I CRIED, LINUS..I CRIED AND CRIED AND CRIED!
YOU'D BETTER GIVE ME MY BLANKET BACK...I DON'T THINK I'M READY FOR THIS...

Z
I'M AWAKE! I'M AWAKE!

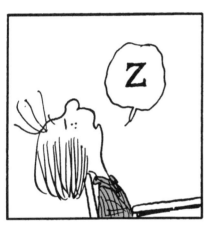

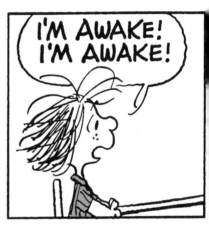

NO, MA'AM...I DON'T KNOW WHAT'S GOING ON
BUT I'M AWAKE!

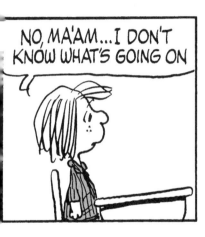

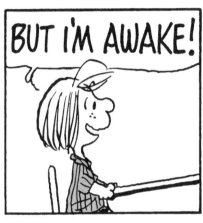

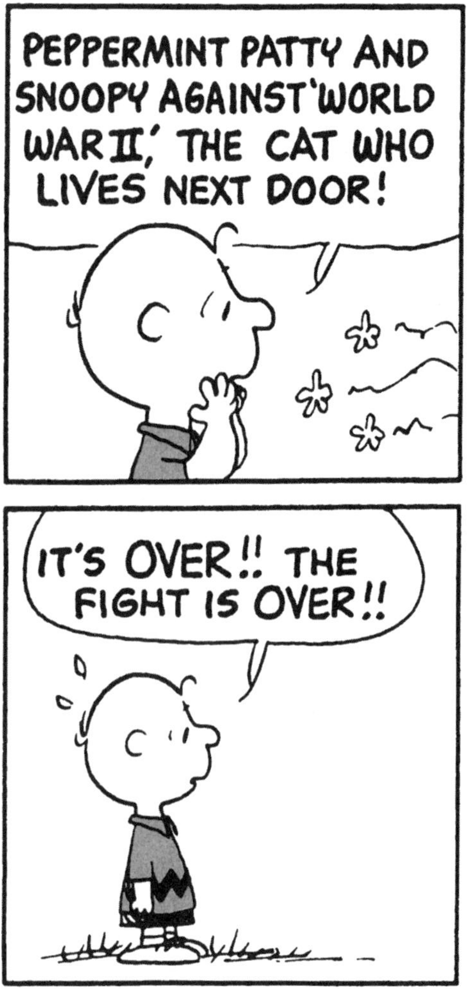
PEPPERMINT PATTY AND SNOOPY AGAINST 'WORLD WAR II,' THE CAT WHO LIVES NEXT DOOR!
IT'S OVER!! THE FIGHT IS OVER!!

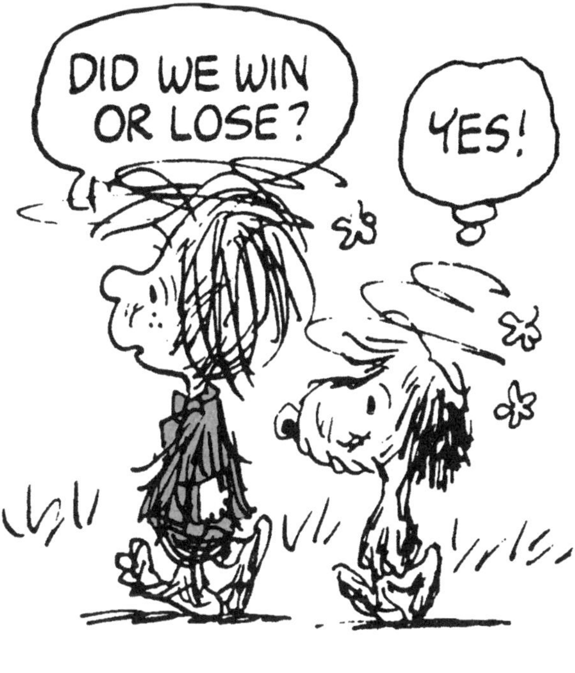
DID WE WIN OR LOSE?
YES!

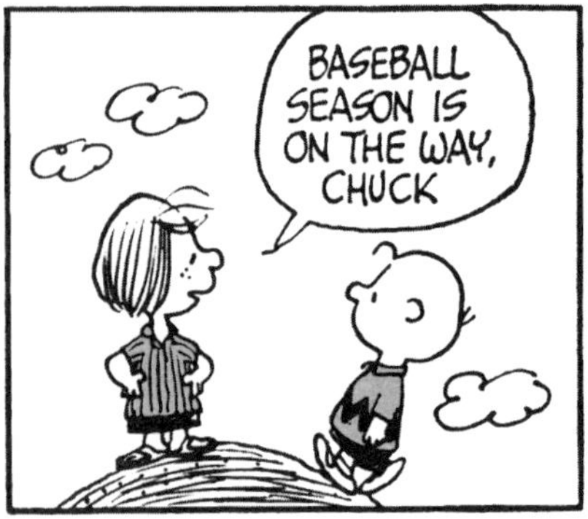
BASEBALL SEASON IS ON THE WAY, CHUCK

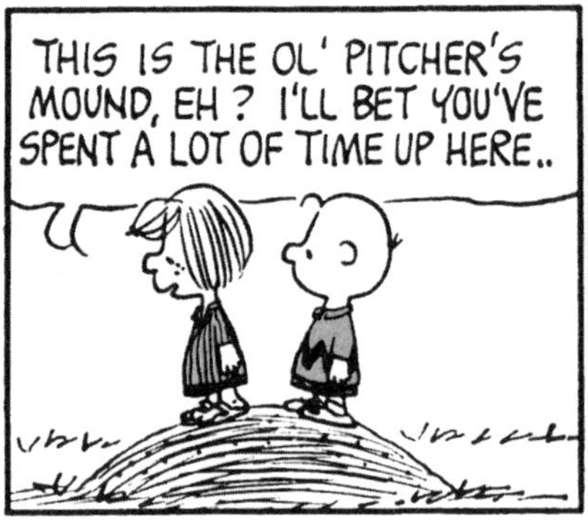
THIS IS THE OL' PITCHER'S MOUND, EH ? I'LL BET YOU'VE SPENT A LOT OF TIME UP HERE..

I LOVE BASEBALL.. I COULD PLAY BASEBALL EVERY DAY OF MY LIFE
YOU'RE AN UNUSUAL GIRL..
YOU KIND OF LIKE ME, DON'T YOU, CHUCK?

OW! OOO! OW!
HOOP HOOP HOOP HOOP

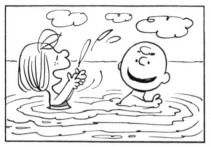

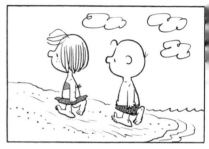

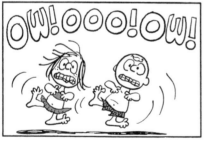

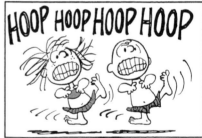

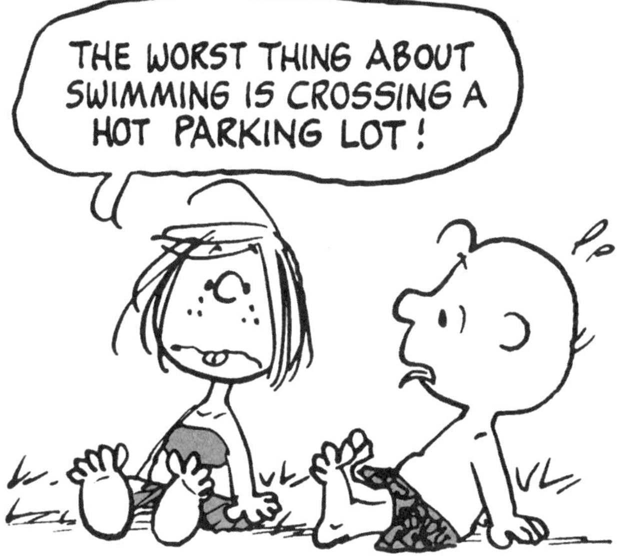
THE WORST THING ABOUT SWIMMING IS CROSSING A HOT PARKING LOT!

THIS IS SOME TEST
"WHO WAS CYRIL FOX? DISCUSS BRIEFLY THE BRONZE AGE"

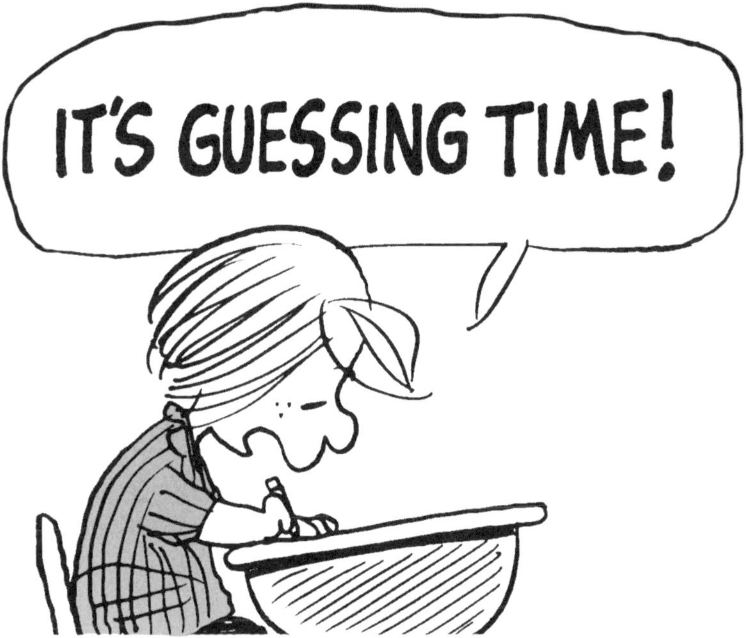
IT'S GUESSING TIME!

I'VE WORKED OUT THE BASEBALL SCHEDULE FOR OUR TWO TEAMS, CHUCK...
HERE, TAKE A LOOK AT IT, AND SEE WHAT YOU THINK..

YOU TOUCHED MY HAND, CHUCK!

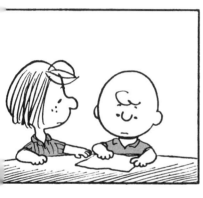

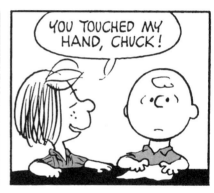

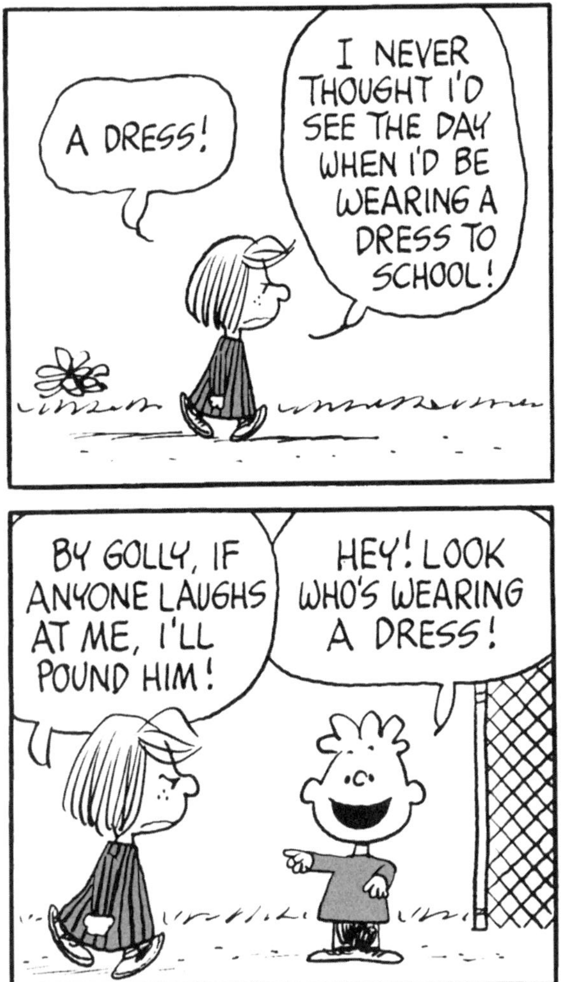
A DRESS!
I NEVER THOUGHT I'D SEE THE DAY WHEN I'D BE WEARING A DRESS TO SCHOOL!
BY GOLLY, IF ANYONE LAUGHS AT ME, I'LL POUND HIM!
HEY! LOOK WHO'S WEARING A DRESS!

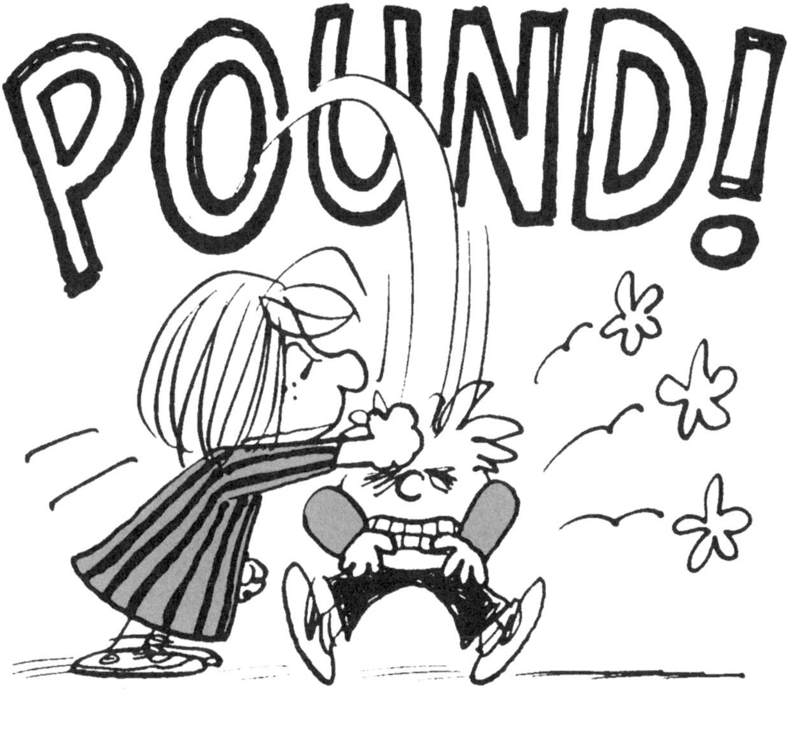
POUND!

THEY SAY IT'S THE SCHOOL DRESS CODE, LINUS..
I CAN'T WEAR MY SANDALS TO SCHOOL ANY MORE... I'M REALLY UPSET... SNIF!

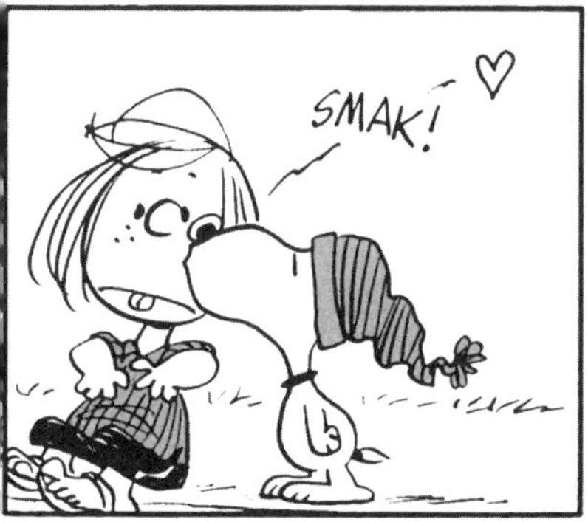
SMAK!

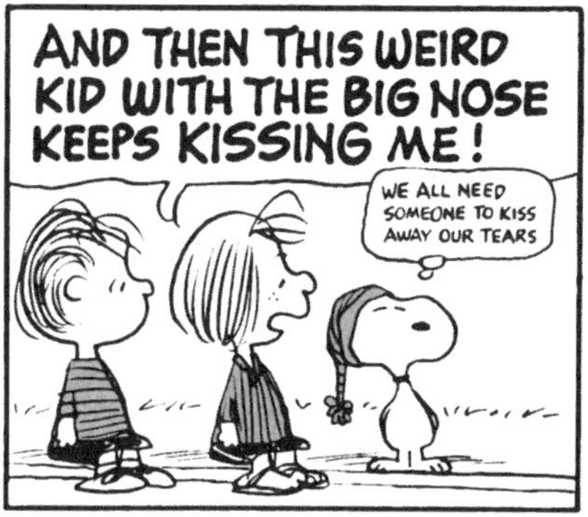
AND THEN THIS WEIRD KID WITH THE BIG NOSE KEEPS KISSING ME!
WE ALL NEED SOMEONE TO KISS AWAY OUR TEARS

A MOVIE, MA'AM?
THAT'S GREAT! I ALWAYS LIKE MOVIES

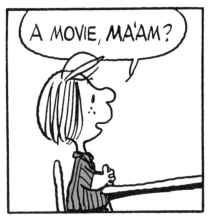

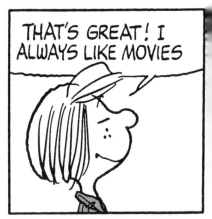

MOVIES IN THE CLASSROOM CAN BE ONE OF OUR BEST LEARNING TOOLS
Z

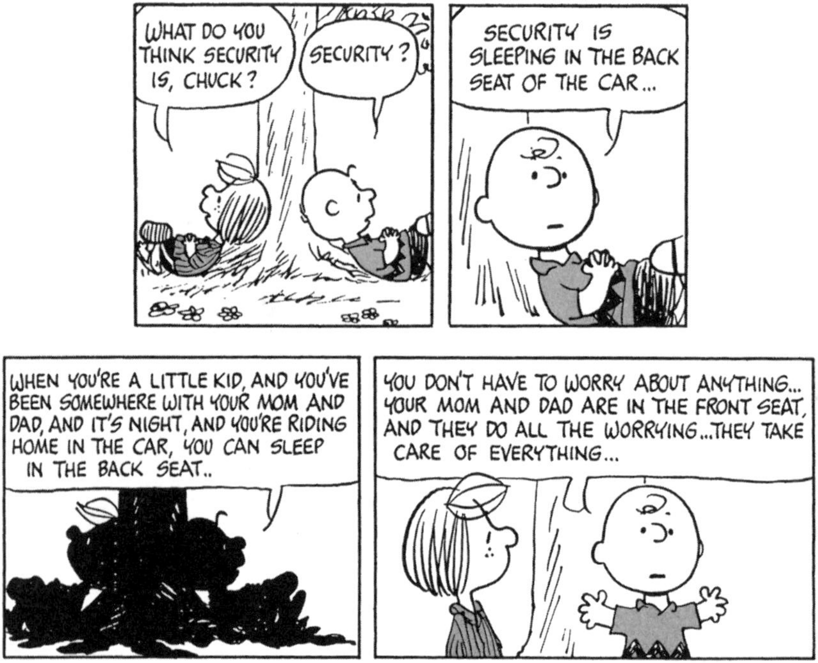
WHAT DO YOU THINK SECURITY IS, CHUCK?
SECURITY?
SECURITY IS SLEEPING IN THE BACK SEAT OF THE CAR...
WHEN YOU'RE A LITTLE KID, AND YOU'VE BEEN SOMEWHERE WITH YOUR MOM AND DAD, AND IT'S NIGHT, AND YOU'RE RIDING HOME IN THE CAR, YOU CAN SLEEP IN THE BACK SEAT..
YOU DON'T HAVE TO WORRY ABOUT ANYTHING... YOUR MOM AND DAD ARE IN THE FRONT SEAT, AND THEY DO ALL THE WORRYING...THEY TAKE CARE OF EVERYTHING...

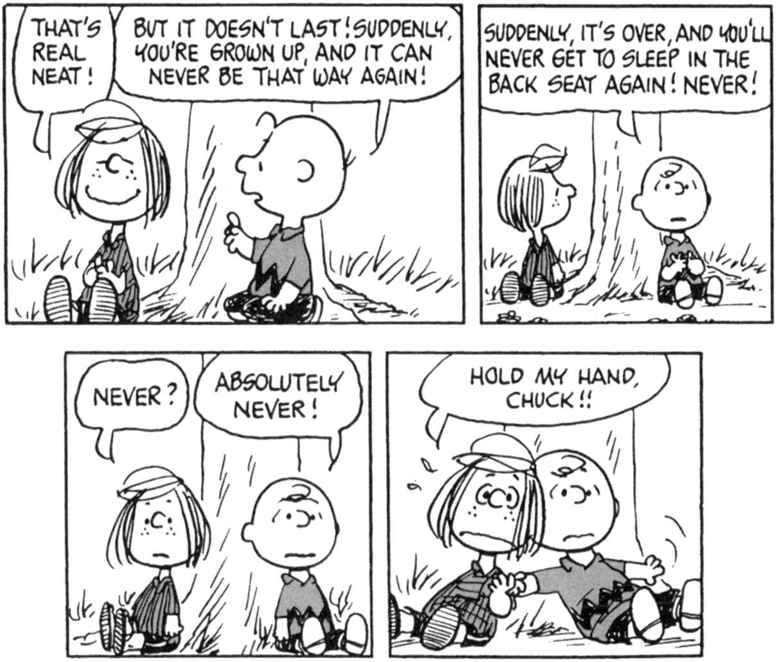
THAT'S REAL NEAT!
BUT IT DOESN'T LAST! SUDDENLY, YOU'RE GROWN UP, AND IT CAN NEVER BE THAT WAY AGAIN!
SUDDENLY, IT'S OVER, AND YOU'LL NEVER GET TO SLEEP IN THE BACK SEAT AGAIN! NEVER!
NEVER?
ABSOLUTELY NEVER!
HOLD MY HAND, CHUCK!!

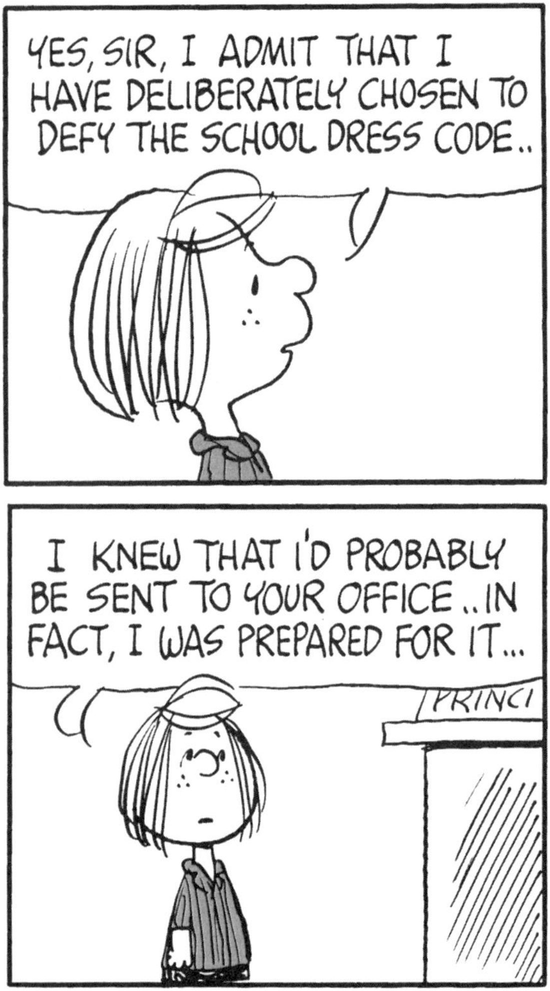
YES, SIR, I ADMIT THAT I HAVE DELIBERATELY CHOSEN TO DEFY THE SCHOOL DRESS CODE..
I KNEW THAT I'D PROBABLY BE SENT TO YOUR OFFICE..IN FACT, I WAS PREPARED FOR IT...
PRINCI

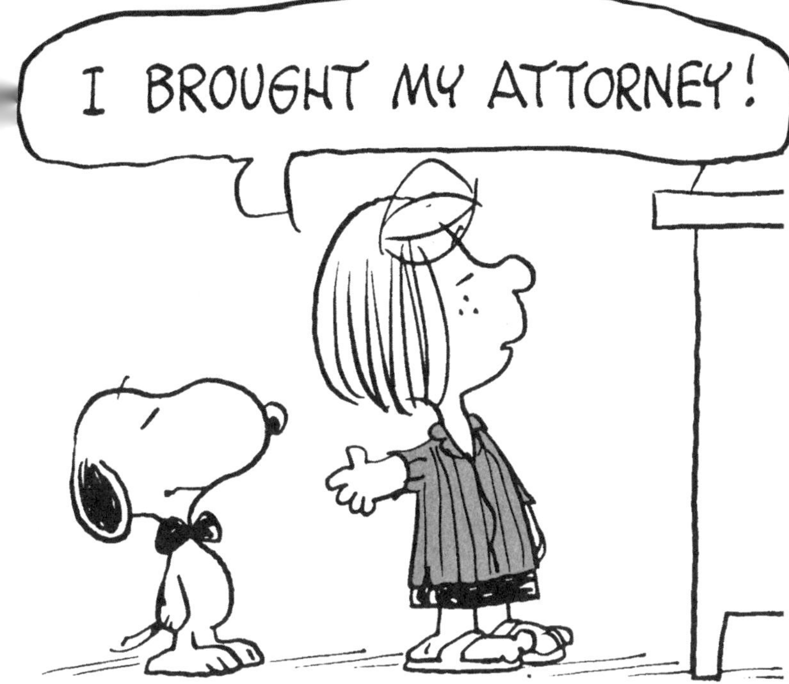
I BROUGHT MY ATTORNEY!

LINUS, IF A PERSON LIKES ANOTHER PERSON, BUT THAT OTHER PERSON DOESN'T LIKE THE FIRST PERSON AS MUCH AS THAT FIRST PERSON LIKES THE OTHER PERSON, WHAT SHOULD THE OTHER PERSON DO?
SAY THAT AGAIN
IF A PERSON LIKES ANOTHER PERSON, BUT THAT OTHER PERSON DOESN'T LIKE THE FIRST PERSON AS MUCH AS THAT FIRST PERSON LIKES THE OTHER PERSON, WHAT SHOULD THE OTHER PERSON DO?

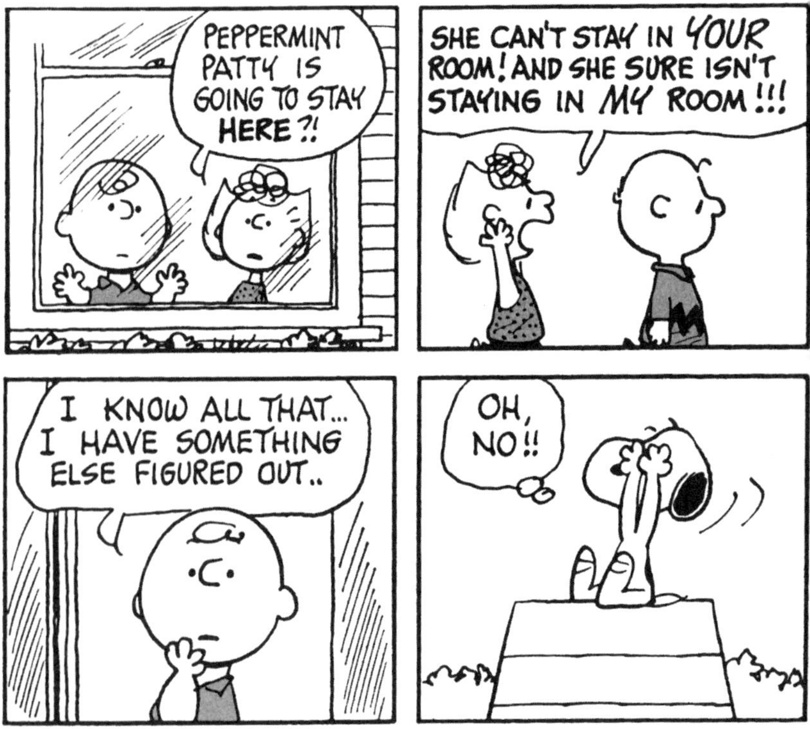
PEPPERMINT PATTY IS GOING TO STAY HERE?!
SHE CAN'T STAY IN YOUR ROOM! AND SHE SURE ISN'T STAYING IN MY ROOM!!!
I KNOW ALL THAT... I HAVE SOMETHING ELSE FIGURED OUT..
OH, NO!!

GOOD GRIEF!
TIME TO GET UP FOR SCHOOL, PATTY!
SORRY FOR THE WAY I LOOK, MA'AM... BLAME IT ON THE STUPID ARCHITECT WHO DESIGNED CHUCK'S GUEST COTTAGE!

OKAY, CHUCK, THIS IS THE WAY WE'RE GONNA WORK..
AS LONG AS WE'RE SITTING AT THE SAME DESK, WE MIGHT AS WELL BE A TEAM...

!
YOUR HIP IS TOUCHING MY HIP, CHUCK!

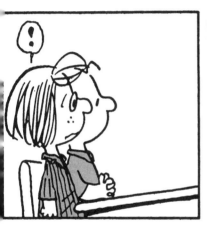

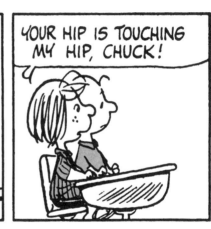

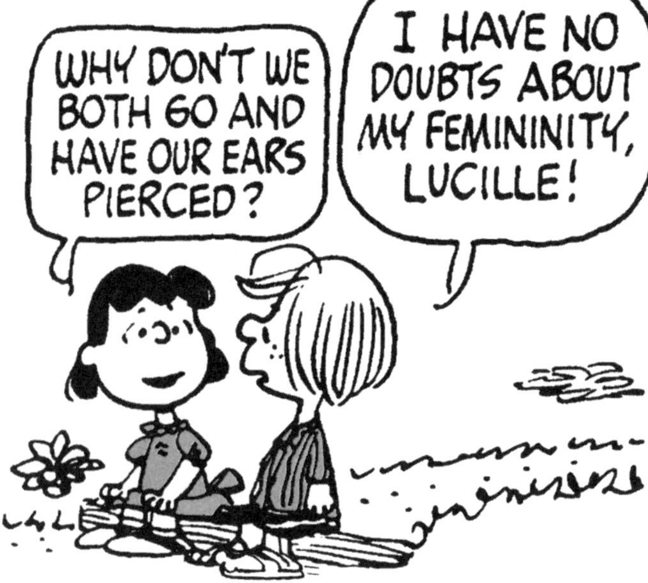
WHY DON'T WE BOTH GO AND HAVE OUR EARS PIERCED?
I HAVE NO DOUBTS ABOUT MY FEMININITY, LUCILLE!

I'D LIKE TO HAVE MY EARS PIERCED, BUT I'M AFRAID IT WILL HURT
IT PROBABLY DOESN'T HURT ANY MORE THAN A PUNCH IN THE NOSE
WHO WANTS TO GET PUNCHED IN THE NOSE?
THAT'S HOW I JUDGE PAIN, LUCILLE... THAT'S HOW I DECIDE WHETHER OR NOT I SHOULD DO SOMETHING...
WILL IT HURT MORE THAN A PUNCH IN THE NOSE OR LESS THAN A PUNCH IN THE NOSE?

TRUE! FALSE! TRUE!
TRUE! FALSE! FALSE! TRUE! FALSE! FALSE! TRUE! FALSE!

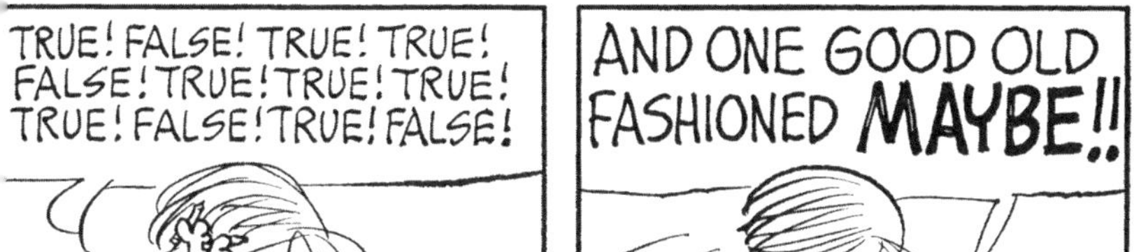
TRUE! FALSE! TRUE! TRUE! FALSE! TRUE! TRUE! TRUE! TRUE! FALSE! TRUE! FALSE!
AND ONE GOOD OLD FASHIONED MAYBE!!

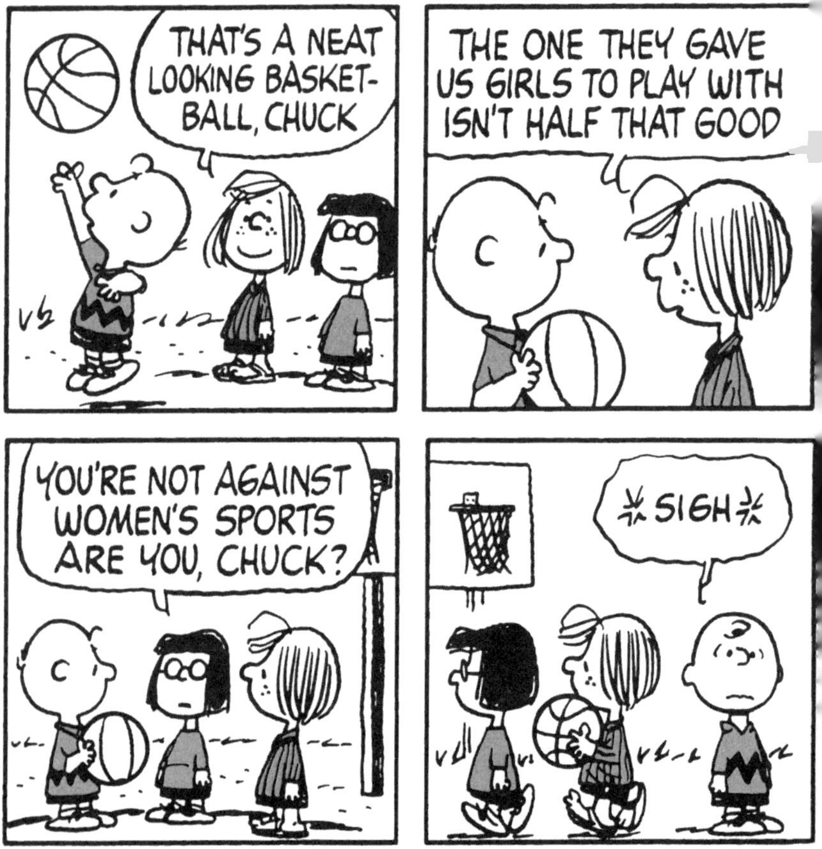
THAT'S A NEAT LOOKING BASKET-BALL, CHUCK
THE ONE THEY GAVE US GIRLS TO PLAY WITH ISN'T HALF THAT GOOD
YOU'RE NOT AGAINST WOMEN'S SPORTS ARE YOU, CHUCK?
SIGH

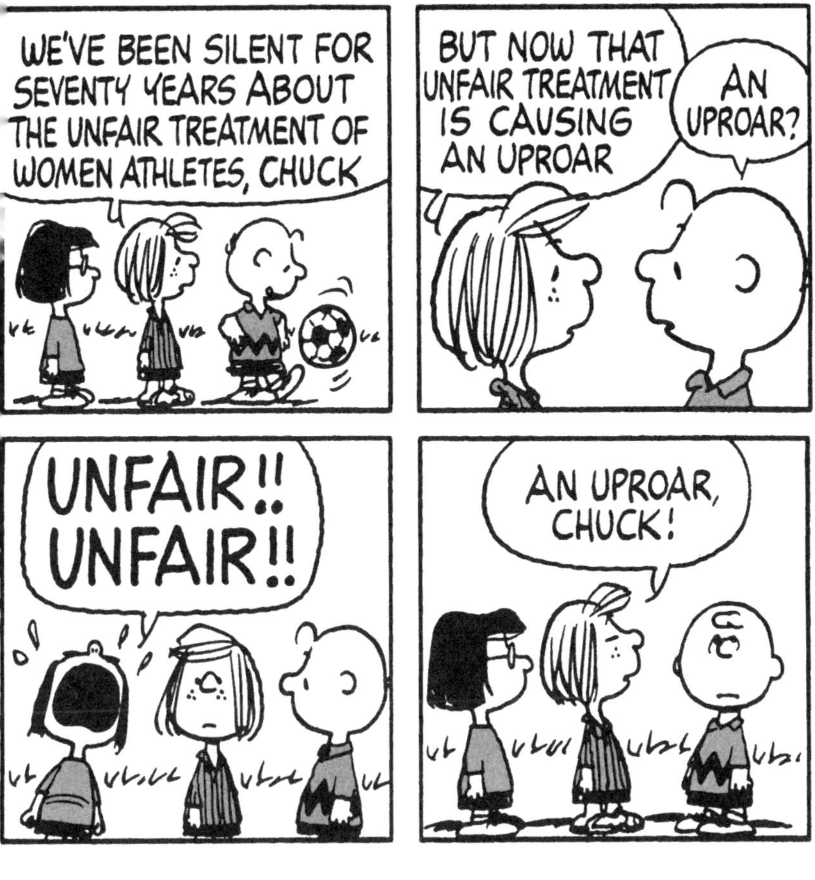
WE'VE BEEN SILENT FOR SEVENTY YEARS ABOUT THE UNFAIR TREATMENT OF WOMEN ATHLETES, CHUCK
BUT NOW THAT UNFAIR TREATMENT IS CAUSING AN UPROAR
AN UPROAR?
UNFAIR!! UNFAIR!!
AN UPROAR, CHUCK!

ALL RIGHT, MARCIE...WHAT BOOK SHOULD I READ?
HOW ABOUT ONE BY KATHERINE ANNE PORTER, OR JOYCE CAROL OATES OR PAMELA HANSFORD JOHNSON?

FORGET IT, MARCIE... ALL THOSE AUTHORS HAVE THREE NAMES...

BY THE TIME I FINISHED READING THE AUTHOR'S NAME, I'D BE TOO TIRED TO READ THE BOOK!

YOU'RE REALLY WEIRD, SIR!

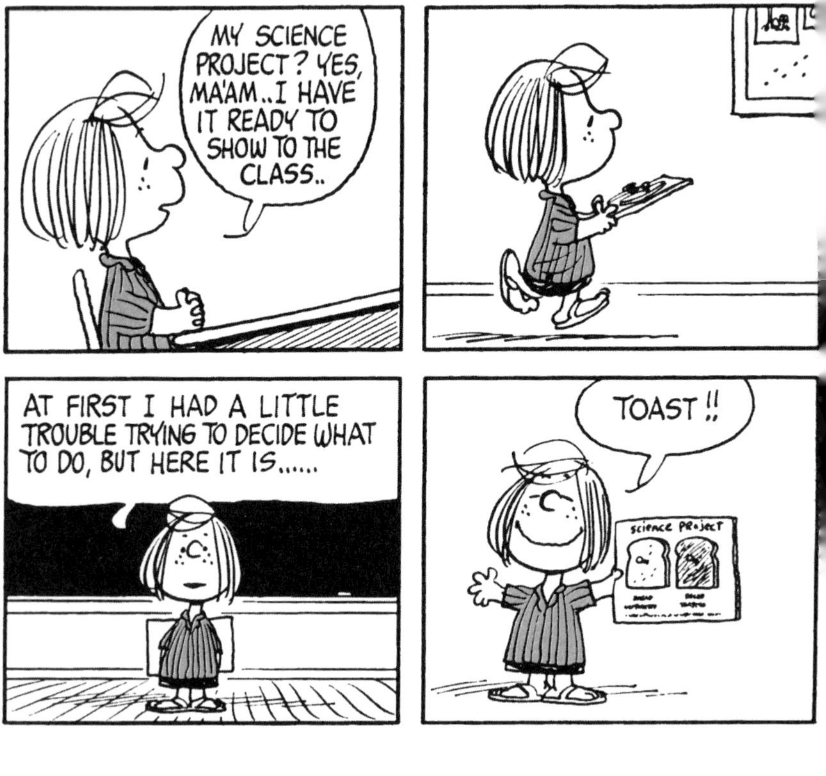
MY SCIENCE PROJECT? YES, MA'AM..I HAVE IT READY TO SHOW TO THE CLASS..
AT FIRST I HAD A LITTLE TROUBLE TRYING TO DECIDE WHAT TO DO, BUT HERE IT IS.....
TOAST!!
SCIENCE PROJECT

MY SCIENCE PROJECT IS TOAST... NOW, HERE ON THIS BOARD IS A SLICE OF UNTOASTED BREAD AND..
HA HA HA HA HA HA
HA HA HA HA
HA HA HA HA
POW!!
I HATE SCIENCE PROJECTS
PRINCIPAL'S OFFICE

HEY, CHUCK, COME ON OVER, AND SEE WHAT MY DAD GAVE ME FOR MY BIRTHDAY..
ROSES!
WOW!
HE SAID THAT I'M GROWING UP FAST, AND SOON I'LL BE A BEAUTIFUL YOUNG LADY, AND ALL THE BOYS WILL BE CALLING ME UP SO HE JUST WANTED TO BE THE FIRST ONE IN MY LIFE TO GIVE ME A DOZEN ROSES!
HE CALLS ME "A RARE GEM"
YOUR DAD LIKES YOU... HAPPY BIRTHDAY..

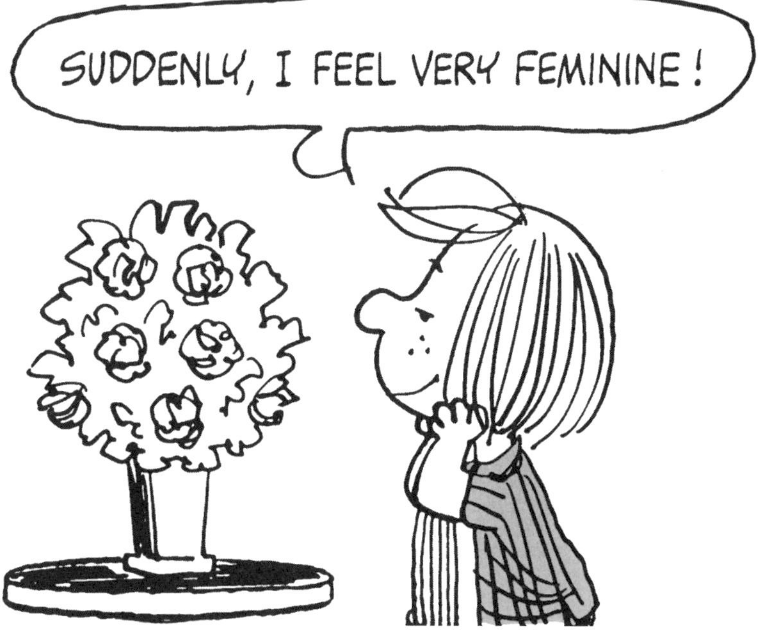
SUDDENLY, I FEEL VERY FEMININE!

PSST, SIR! WAKE UP!
Z
BONK!

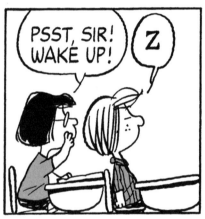

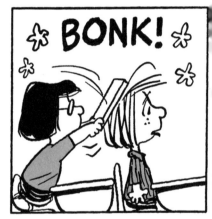

I'M AWAKE! THE ANSWER IS "BONK"
NICE TRY, SIR!

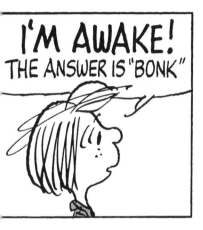

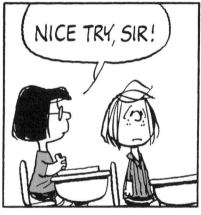

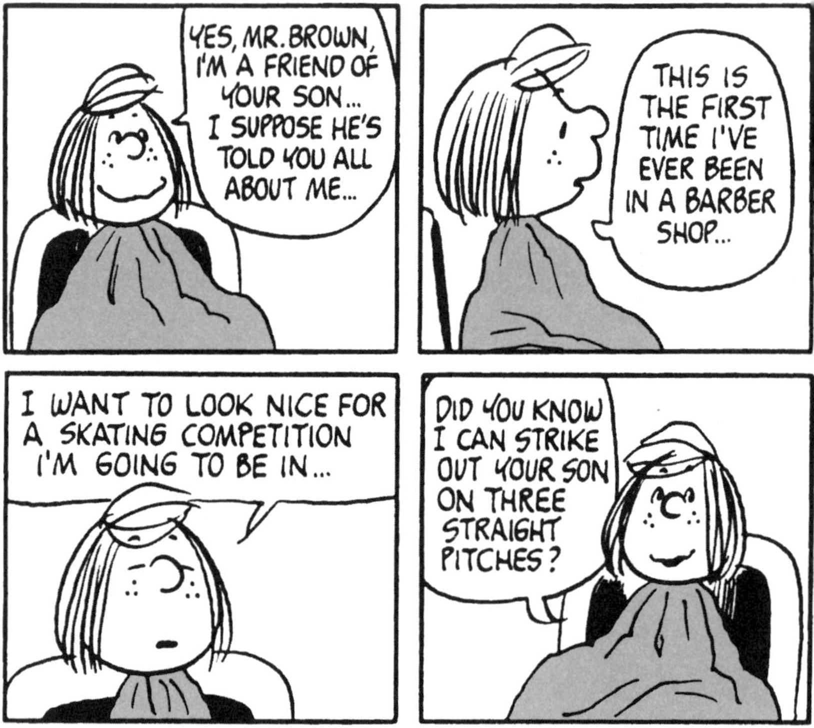
YES, MR. BROWN, I'M A FRIEND OF YOUR SON... I SUPPOSE HE'S TOLD YOU ALL ABOUT ME...
THIS IS THE FIRST TIME I'VE EVER BEEN IN A BARBER SHOP...
I WANT TO LOOK NICE FOR A SKATING COMPETITION I'M GOING TO BE IN...
DID YOU KNOW I CAN STRIKE OUT YOUR SON ON THREE STRAIGHT PITCHES?

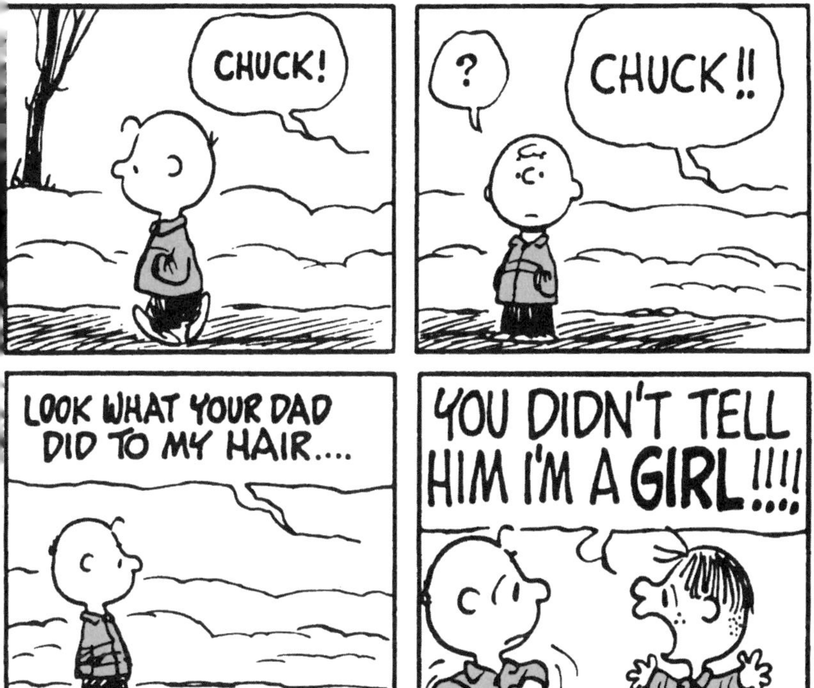
CHUCK!
?
CHUCK!!
LOOK WHAT YOUR DAD DID TO MY HAIR....
YOU DIDN'T TELL HIM I'M A GIRL!!!!

THE BARBER THOUGHT YOU WERE A BOY? THAT'S TERRIBLE, SIR!
A **WIG**? YOU BOUGHT A **WIG**? THAT'S A GREAT IDEA, SIR! NO, I PROMISE NOT TO LAUGH...
NO, I PROMISE... I REALLY DO.. I PROMISE... YES, I REALLY PROMISE... YES, I PROMISE NOT TO LAUGH... YES, SIR, I REALLY, REALLY PROMISE...

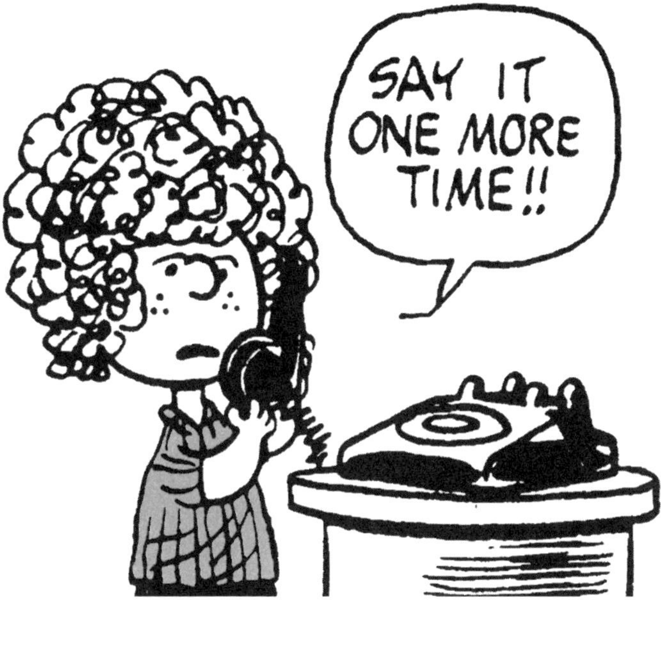
SAY IT ONE MORE TIME!!

MY DAD SAYS THAT I AM "A RARE GEM"
I AGREE WITH HIM
YOU KIND OF LIKE ME, DON'T YOU, CHUCK? I'M GLAD YOU DON'T COME RIGHT OUT AND SAY IT, THOUGH...I RESPECT YOU FOR THAT

THAT'S ALL I NEED... "RESPECT" *SIGH*
WHAT DID YOU SAY, CHUCK? DON'T MUMBLE..
I SAID, "YOU ARE A RARE GEM"
YOU KIND OF LIKE ME, DON'T YOU, CHUCK?

NOW, THAT'S WHAT I CALL A BOOK REPORT..
THIS TIME I REALLY OUTDID MYSELF

I'VE GOT THE AUTHOR'S NAME, A BRIEF DESCRIPTION OF THE PLOT AND EVERYTHING...
I EVEN READ THE BOOK!

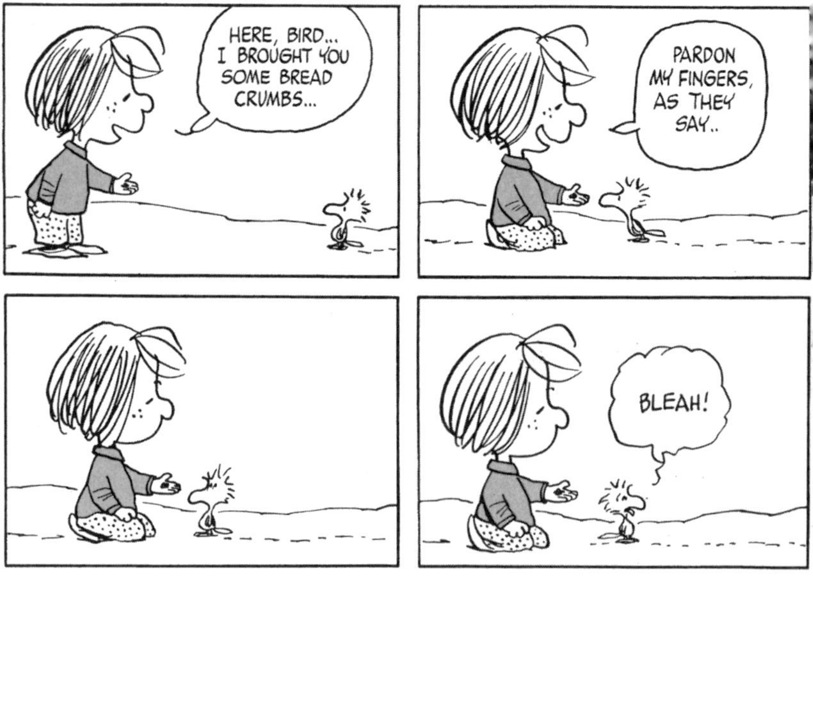
HERE, BIRD... I BROUGHT YOU SOME BREAD CRUMBS...
PARDON MY FINGERS, AS THEY SAY..
BLEAH!

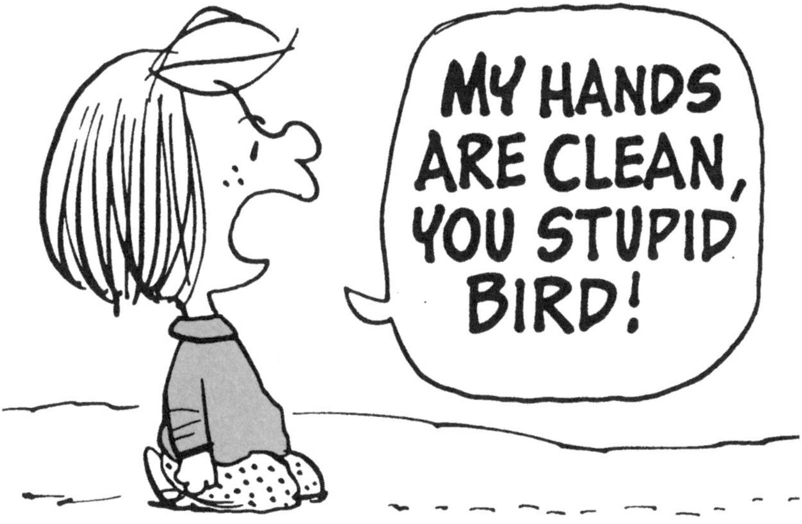
MY HANDS ARE CLEAN, YOU STUPID BIRD!

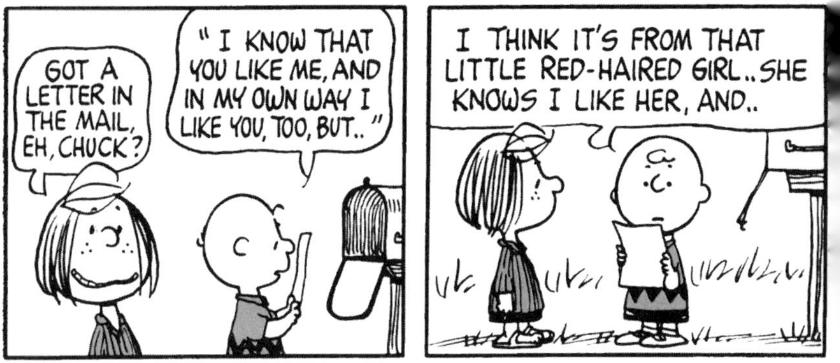
GOT A LETTER IN THE MAIL, EH, CHUCK?
"I KNOW THAT YOU LIKE ME, AND IN MY OWN WAY I LIKE YOU, TOO, BUT.."
I THINK IT'S FROM THAT LITTLE RED-HAIRED GIRL..SHE KNOWS I LIKE HER, AND..

THAT'S NOT FROM ANY LITTLE RED-HAIRED GIRL, CHUCK! THAT LETTER IS FROM ME! YOU LIKE ME, CHUCK!
I DO?

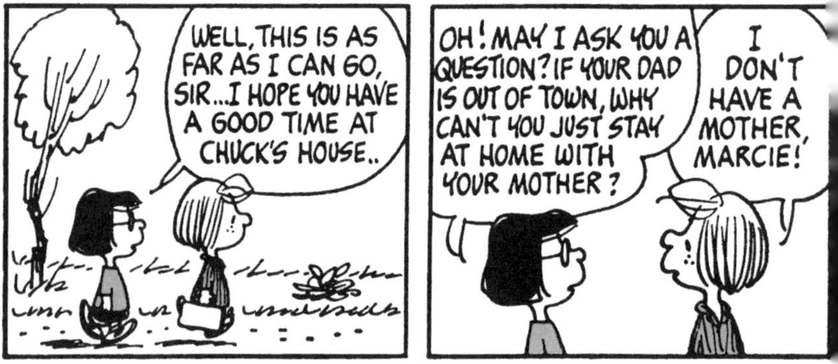
WELL, THIS IS AS FAR AS I CAN GO, SIR...I HOPE YOU HAVE A GOOD TIME AT CHUCK'S HOUSE..
OH! MAY I ASK YOU A QUESTION? IF YOUR DAD IS OUT OF TOWN, WHY CAN'T YOU JUST STAY AT HOME WITH YOUR MOTHER?
I DON'T HAVE A MOTHER, MARCIE!

I THINK I'LL GO HOME, AND PAINT MY TONGUE BLACK!

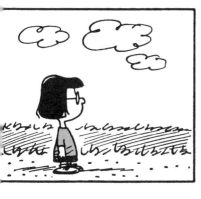

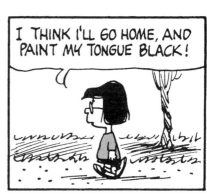

MA'AM, I THINK YOU SHOULD GRADE US ON A CURVE...
THE WAY I SEE IT, THAT'S THE ONLY CHANCE I HAVE TO PASS...
IF I CAN FIND SOMEONE WHO KNOWS LESS THAN I DO, THEN I WON'T BE AT THE BOTTOM OF THE CURVE, RIGHT? RIGHT!!
WELL, I'VE FOUND HIM...

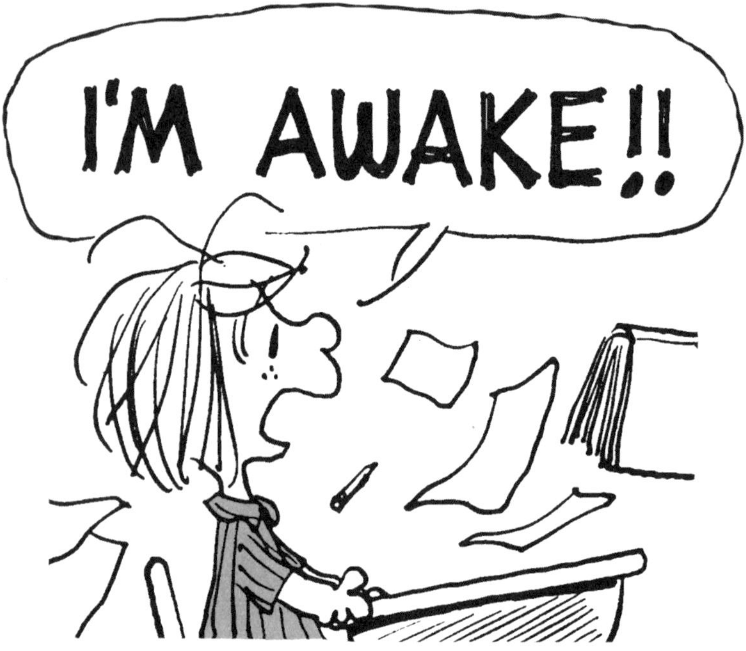
I'M AWAKE!!

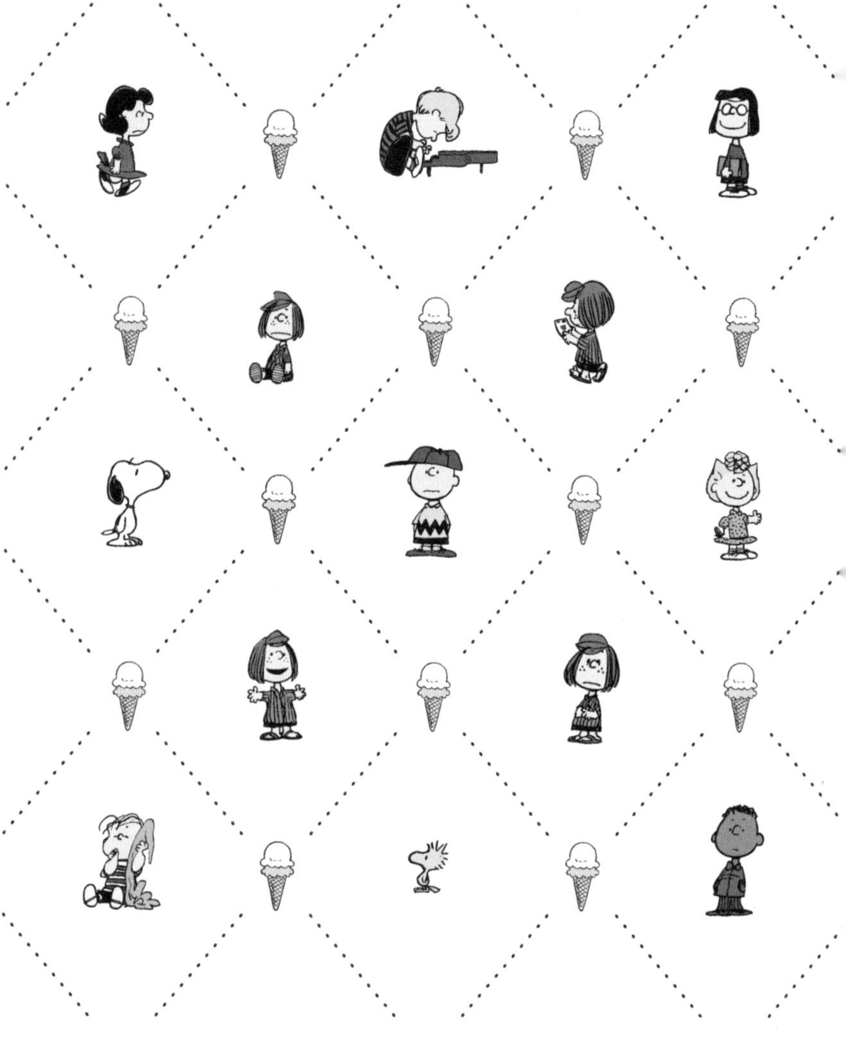